Unbelievable Pictures and Facts About Uganda

By: Olivia Greenwood

Introduction

Uganda is a country that is home to many mountain gorillas. People from all over the world come to Uganda to go gorilla trekking. Now is your chance to learn everything that you need to know about the fascinating country of Uganda.

Should you tip people in Uganda?

It is customary and considered to be good manners to tip people in Uganda. You can tip the waiter, a tour guide and a car driver. They will really appreciate any tips that you give them.

Which religion do people practice the most in Uganda?

The most practiced religion in the country of Uganda is Christianity.

What is the culture like in Uganda?

Uganda has a very mixed culture. The country is made up of all different ethnic groups and languages. People are usually friendly and you will find different people from all walks of life.

Is it expensive to buy things in Uganda?

If you are coming from a different country, it usually is very cheap to buy things in Uganda. With the currency conversion rate and other factors, things in Uganda are generally very cheap for tourists.

Are the people in Uganda friendly to tourists?

The people in Uganda are really kind. Helpful and friendly towards tourists. The good news is that many of the people in Uganda can speak English.

What type of landscape does Uganda have?

Uganda has a landscape that is filled with mountains, rivers, valleys, parks, forests and lots of wildlife.

Do many people come to Uganda to do charity work?

People come from all over the world to do charity work in Uganda. Uganda really relies on the kindness of people doing charity to work, to help them.

Are there many orphans in Uganda?

Unfortunately, Uganda is a country that is home to many orphans. One of the biggest problems in Uganda is the HIV virus. Unfortunately, babies lose their parents very early on in life. There are many children in Uganda who are looking to get adopted.

Are any products made in Uganda?

There are many products which are made in Uganda. Some products include coffee, fish, maize, tobacco, flowers, and cotton.

What type of weather do they have in Uganda?

The weather in Uganda can change quite quickly. One moment it can be raining and the next minute the sun will be shining. The weather is quite unpredictable and weather patterns change quite often.

Will you find any mountains in Uganda?

You will find many mountains in the country of Uganda.

What language do people in the country of Uganda speak?

There are two main languages which people in the country of Uganda speak. These languages are Swahili and English.

Can you go on a safari in Uganda?

You certainly can go on a safari if you find yourself in Uganda. There are many fantastic safari tours which are offered all over the country.

Will you find any animals in Uganda?

You will find many impressive animals all over Uganda. There are also over 100 different birds. You will also find tons of gorillas, more than anywhere in the world.

What is the population amount in Uganda?

There are currently over 43 million people living in Uganda. This amount constantly changes each and every year.

What financial currency do people use to buy things with?

If you want to buy things in Uganda, you will need to know what currency they make use of. The financial currency which they make use of in Uganda is the Ugandan shilling.

Is the country of Uganda rich or poor?

Unfortunately, Uganda is a poor country. The country has suffered many hardships throughout the years.

Is Uganda a landlocked country?

The answer is yes, Uganda certainly is a landlocked country.

What city is the capital one in the country?

The name of the capital city of Uganda is Kampala.

Where in the world will you find Uganda?

Do you know how to find East-Central Africa on the map? This is where you will be able to find Uganda. You can also look for Rwanda, South Sudan or Kenya and you will find Uganda in no time.

Printed in Great Britain
by Amazon